Sandra Markle

The Case of the Vanishing Little Brown Bats

A Scientific Mystery

M Millbrook Press . Minneapolis

For good friends George
and Muriel Warren

Acknowledgments: The author would like to thank the following people for taking the time to share their expertise: Dr. Melissa Behr, University of Wisconsin; Dr. David Blehert, United States Geological Survey National Wildlife Health Center; Dr. Paul Cryan, United States Geologic Survey-Fort Collins Science Center; Dr. Winifred Frick, University of California, Santa Cruz; Nathan Fuller, Boston University; Carl Herzog, New York State Department of Environmental Conservation; Alan Hicks, New York State Department of Environmental Conservation (retired); Kate Langwig, Boston University; Dr. Carol Meteyer, United States Geological Survey National Center, Contaminant Biology Program; and Dr. DeeAnn Reeder, Bucknell University. A special thank-you to Skip Jeffery for his loving support during the creative process.

Pronunciation guide for *Pseudogymnoascus destructans* on p. 26 provided by Dr. David Blehert.

Millbrook Press
A division of Lerner Publishing Group, Inc.
241 First Avenue North
Minneapolis, MN 55401 USA

For reading levels and more information, look up this title at www.lernerbooks.com.

Main body text set in Johnston ITC Std. 14/21.
Typeface provided by International Typeface Corp.

Library of Congress Cataloging-in-Publication Data

Markle, Sandra.
    The case of the vanishing little brown bats: A scientific mystery / Sandra Markle.
        pages cm
    Includes index.
    ISBN 978–1–4677–1463–1 (lib. bdg. : alk. paper)
    ISBN 978–1–4677–4765–3 (eBook)
    1. Little brown bat—Juvenile literature. 2. White-nose syndrome—Research—Juvenile literature.
    3. Little brown bat—Diseases—Research—Juvenile literature. I. Title.
    QL737.C595M365 2015
    595.77'4—dc23   2013030953

Manufactured in the United States of America
1 – DP – 7/15/14

Table of Contents

It's a Mystery

On a cold winter day in 2011, bat researcher Kate Langwig discovered something exciting in the Adirondack Mountains. Deep inside an abandoned mine, she found a little brown bat.

Once, finding a little brown bat in this mine would have been nothing special. Each year, dark, cool caverns in the area became the winter homes for about two hundred thousand bats. Most of those were a type of bat known as the little brown bat. The bats came to the caves to hibernate, or go into an inactive state. Bats hibernate while temperatures are too cold for them to survive and the bats' main food is unavailable. However, hibernation is no longer a sure way for bats to survive the winter. In recent years, something that strikes only during winter is killing bats—lots of them.

Kate Langwig checks on a little brown bat. The body of a full-grown little brown bat is only about 2 inches (5 centimeters) long.

Little brown bats have been especially hard hit by this mysterious killer. They were once among the most common kinds of bats in North America. But by 2013, their numbers had dropped so much that scientists wondered whether the bats should be listed as an endangered species (a species in serious danger of becoming extinct, or gone forever).

Losing bats, especially little brown bats, could have disastrous effects for both nature and people. That's because these bats are insect eaters. Insects do serious damage to crops. They can also transmit diseases, such as West Nile virus, to people and other animals. So, higher numbers of insects could spread diseases at a higher rate.

Clearly, little brown bats are a valuable part of our ecosystem.

Little brown bats may eat as much as half their weight in insects on a summer night.

Bats in Trouble!

Scientists first realized on March 17, 2007, that bats were dying in large numbers.

That day a team from the New York State Department of Environmental Conservation went to Hailes Cave, near Albany, New York. Once a year during the winter, researchers from this organization went into area caves to count the hibernating bats. It's how they check on bat populations. That year, the first thing that surprised the team was seeing bats swooping through the air outside the cave when they should have been inside hibernating. Then the team reached the cave and discovered the bodies of dead bats—lots of them. The team collected some of the dead bats. They also took photos of others that were alive but strangely awake instead of hibernating.

Back at headquarters, Al Hicks, the conservation team's director, was stunned by the team's report. He was

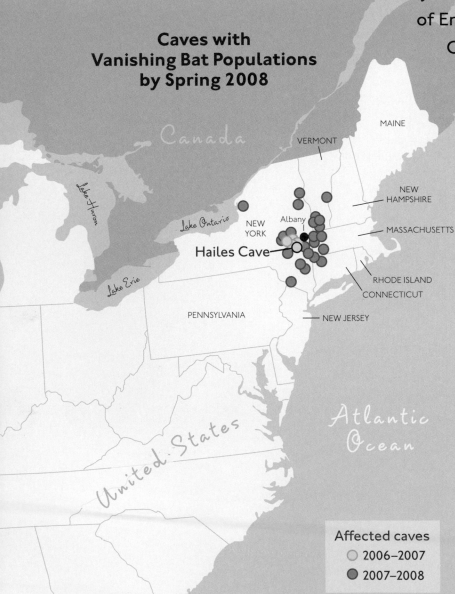

Caves with Vanishing Bat Populations by Spring 2008

Canada

Lake Huron

Lake Ontario

Lake Erie

MAINE

VERMONT

NEW YORK

Albany

Hailes Cave

NEW HAMPSHIRE

MASSACHUSETTS

RHODE ISLAND

CONNECTICUT

NEW JERSEY

PENNSYLVANIA

United States

Atlantic Ocean

Affected caves
○ 2006–2007
● 2007–2008

also amazed by one of the photos. It showed little brown bats with white fuzz on their noses. "In nearly thirty years of studying bats," he said, "I'd never seen anything like those bats with white noses."

Hicks quickly e-mailed the photo to other New York bat survey teams. He asked if anyone had seen what his team discovered. Everyone had just completed their winter surveys, but they went back to check sites again. The teams found hibernating little brown and other kinds of bats with fuzzy white noses in four caves near Hailes Cave. They didn't find dead bats, though.

In 2006 the Hailes Cave survey showed this site sheltered sixteen thousand hibernating bats. In 2007 the winter population was estimated to be only eleven hundred bats.

This is the very first photo ever taken of bats with fuzzy white noses.

Scientists puzzled over the mystery of the dead bats. It remained unsolved when the weather warmed and the surviving bats became active. However, those bats appeared healthy. Whatever had happened was chalked up to a one-time event. In fact, nothing seemed out of the ordinary until the next winter. In January 2008, local residents near Albany, New York, spotted bats flying during a snowstorm. Again, bats that should have been hibernating were awake. Al Hicks assembled a team and went to investigate. The number of dead bats and skeletons he discovered in one cave shocked him. Hicks packaged up some of the dead bats and sent them to the US Geological Survey National Wildlife Health Center (NWHC) in Wisconsin.

More bad news followed. That winter large numbers of dead bats were discovered at eighteen sites in New York plus sites in Vermont, Massachusetts, and Connecticut. Then spring arrived and once again, the surviving bats returned to life as usual. But scientists now knew that something was terribly wrong. And the problem was clearly spreading. Something had to be done—fast. First, though, scientists needed to figure out what was killing the bats.

The bodies of the dead bats decomposed (broke down), leaving only bones behind on the cave floor.

What Is Killing the Bats?

When scientists are racing against time to solve a mystery such as this, they tackle it from several angles at once. They look at different possible causes of the problem so they can more quickly find a way to stop it.

Could Climate Change Be the Problem?

Could bats be dying because of rising temperatures? In recent years, scientists have observed changes in the climate (the average weather of a place over time) in many places around the globe. Recorded average temperatures have been warming. To hibernate, bats need their environment to stay cool, between 35°F and 50°F (2°C and 10°C). Any warmer and bats become active and need to eat.

Healthy little brown bats usually live at least ten years. They often hibernate in the same site—even the same crack or crevice—each year.

What Do Hibernating Bats Need?

A hibernating bat needs to be undisturbed. Coming out of hibernation causes it to use up stored body fat as it warms up and becomes active.

Hibernating is all about surviving without having to eat when there isn't any food available. When a bat goes into hibernation, its heart rate slows from about four hundred beats per minute to as few as twenty-five beats per minute. Its breathing rate also slows. Blood flow to its feet and wings greatly decreases. Its body temperature drops from about 94°F (34°C) to just above freezing. Then a bat slowly uses its stored body fat to stay alive. However, even during hibernation, a bat continues to lose water. Mainly, moisture evaporates through its nearly naked wings. That causes its body to dehydrate (dry out) enough that it arouses every couple of weeks. The bat's body takes nearly an hour to warm up to be ready to fly. Then the bat flies to get a drink of water and pass liquid wastes before returning to its hibernation site. Within about twenty minutes of settling down, the bat is back to hibernating again.

Hibernating close together can help bats stay warmer and save energy. However, when one bat becomes active, it bumps and disturbs the others.

Weather records showed that air temperatures outside the caves and mines where bats hibernate in New York State had increased over the past thirty years. Some scientists feared the hibernation sites could be heating up inside too, causing bats to become active when insects are unavailable. Then the bats could be starving to death.

But New York bat researchers had proof that wasn't true. For twenty-five years, in addition to counting the bats each winter, they had recorded each site's temperature and humidity (amount of moisture in the air). Those records showed that these conditions inside the hibernation sites had not changed. So the bats' deaths couldn't be due to climate change.

Could Pesticides Be the Killer?

Some scientists wondered if pesticides could be killing the bats. Many farmers spray these chemicals to kill insect pests. Were bats dying from eating insects coated with chemicals? A group of veterinary pathologists decided to find out. These scientists use lab techniques to figure out what is harming animals. A team at the USGS Patuxent Wildlife Research Center in Maryland tested tissue samples from the dead bats' livers, brains, and kidneys. They discovered the bats' bodies did contain traces of pesticides. Then the researchers tested tissue samples from twenty healthy bats. The healthy bats' tissues contained about the same amount of pesticides. So the scientists concluded that pesticides weren't the reason the bats were dying.

This healthy little brown bat was tested for pesticides. The bat came from Kentucky, well beyond where any bats had died at that point.

Could a Virus Be Killing the Bats?

Some scientists believed a disease must be killing the bats. Carol Meteyer, a pathologist at NWHC, looked for damaged organs in the dead bats. Organ damage would prove the bats had been sick. However, the bats' internal organs looked normal.

Some scientists were still convinced the bats were dying from an infectious disease. But they decided it must be something like human immunodeficiency virus (HIV). This type of disease keeps the body's immune system from working the way it should. Scientists at Columbia University tested tissue samples from the dead bats. They used state-of-the-art technology specially designed to look for viruses, including HIV-type viruses. Those tests ruled out a virus as the mysterious killer.

Carol Meteyer examines
a dead bat in her lab.

What Else Could Be Killing the Bats?

Researchers noticed that many bats that were awake when they should have been hibernating had patches of white fuzz on their bodies. It was particularly on their noses. Al Hicks was suspicious that the white stuff was at least part of the problem. So he sent several living white-nosed bats to the NWHC lab to be studied. However, on the way to the lab, the white fuzz disappeared. The pathologists saw only bare skin in place of fur where the fuzzy white stuff had been. They wanted to find out what, if any, bacteria or fungi was growing on the bats' skin in those spots. So they swabbed the bare patches. Then they cultured each sample. To do this, they wiped the swab on a shallow glass dish coated with a nutrient gel, transferring whatever the swab had picked up from the bat. Next, the dishes were kept at a warm temperature (in this case, 75°F, or 24°C). Most bacteria or fungi that grow on skin leave behind bits that could be encouraged to grow this way. But even using high-powered microscopes, the pathologists didn't find any bacteria or fungi. Something had been growing on the bats inside the caves, but the team was

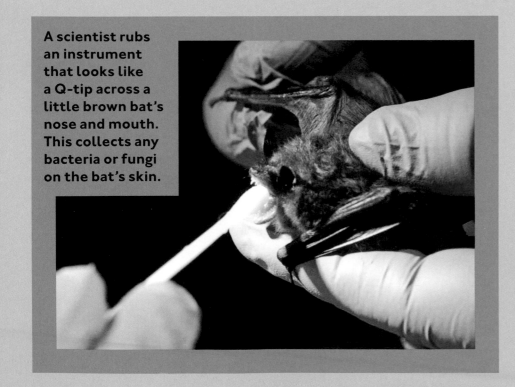

A scientist rubs an instrument that looks like a Q-tip across a little brown bat's nose and mouth. This collects any bacteria or fungi on the bat's skin.

Here in its hibernation site, this bat has white fuzz on its nose. But the fuzz disappeared by the time the bat reached the lab.

A special stain makes the fungus appear bright pink.

unable to get it to grow in the lab. They needed a different way to study it.

Curious, the lab team next cut tissue samples from bare skin patches on the bats' noses and wings. Then they used a microscope to get a highly magnified look. What they discovered was a network of hyphae, the rootlike parts of a fungus. The thread-like structure of the hyphae let them identify the fungus as a type of *Geomyces*. But they were missing the conidia, the seedlike parts that made up the fragile white fuzz. Without it, the scientists couldn't tell exactly what kind of *Geomyces* this particular fungus was.

However, the worst problem any *Geomyces* fungus had been known to cause was a skin condition similar to athlete's foot. No fungus of this type was known to kill. So the lab team concluded the fuzzy white fungus must only be growing on bats that were already sick and dying.

What was killing the bats remained a mystery.

17

Bat Killer Found

All through January 2008, scientist Melissa Behr worked with the NWHC team in Wisconsin, trying to figure out what was killing the bats. She was frustrated that they still hadn't solved this mystery. And she couldn't stop suspecting that the fuzzy white fungus was to blame for the deaths. Behr finally decided that if the fungus couldn't be delivered to her, she'd go to it. So in February, when Al Hicks and his team headed into one of the New York mines where hibernating bats were dying, she went along.

Behr had never conducted tests inside a mine in the middle of winter. In fact, she'd never been inside a cave or a mine in any season. But she was determined to see the white fungus on bats in the field. She hiked through deep snow, climbed down a frozen waterfall, and went into the mine. So many little brown bats had died the year before that not many were

Melissa Behr went into a mine to prepare microscope slides of the white fuzz.

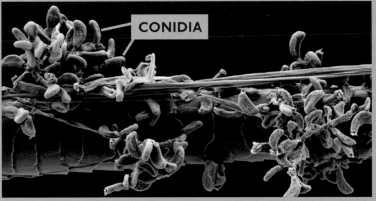

CONIDIA

This is the fungi's conidia, seedlike parts, on a bat hair.

left hibernating in the huge, cold mine. Behr finally found four with fuzzy white noses. One by one, she gently lifted each little brown bat off the rock wall long enough to collect a sample and prepare a slide of the fungus.

Back in her lab, Behr used an electron microscope to take a highly magnified look at the fungi's conidia. It clearly had all the characteristic features of other *Geomyces* fungus. But the conidia of this fungus looked different from any Behr had ever seen before.

These had a unique hooked shape. Behr shared her samples with other scientists. They wondered: Could this fungus be different enough from known *Geomyces* types to be fatal rather than causing a mere skin problem? Might it even be a new kind of fungus and not a *Geomyces* after all?

And whatever it was, could this fungus be what was killing the bats?

The NWHC team needed to culture the new fungus so they could study how it grew. That would help them find out if there was something about this fungus that could be deadly to bats. However, so far, they had been unable to grow the fungus in the lab.

Then the scientists realized where they may have gone wrong. A bat's body temperature during hibernation is only about 43°F (6°C). That's about the same temperature as the inside of a home refrigerator—much cooler than the culturing environment they had tried before. So one of the scientists prepared a fresh culture of the fungus and placed it in the lab's refrigerator. In a little over two weeks, the fungus was growing. The NWHC team could finally study it.

Deep inside, the cave is warmer than the frozen outdoors. But it's still as cool as a refrigerator.

About this time, Melissa Behr visited another mine to collect more samples from the sick bats she found there. When she examined those samples through an electron microscope, she saw the same strange conidia. That proved this new fungus existed in more than one site where bats were dying—places that were far apart. Behr shared these new microscopic views of the fungus. The NWHC scientists could see that the fungus they'd grown in the lab's fridge matched what Behr collected. They suspected this new kind of fungus was involved in the bat deaths. But they couldn't be sure unless they could figure out how the fungus was killing the bats.

Melissa Behr came up with an idea along with Carol Meteyer, who was part of her team. Since this new kind of fungus grew differently, maybe the way it attacked a bat's skin was different too.

The fuzzy white fungus is growing along the edges of a piece of bat wing tissue.

Meteyer went to work to find out. She studied the wing tissue of one of the dead bats. She'd originally thought the patches of bare skin on the wings had suffered only surface damage. After all, the fungus attacking bats was believed to be a kind of *Geomyces*. And that kind of fungus was known to attack only a host's outer skin cells, which are already dead. But Meteyer discovered this new kind of fungus did something much worse. With a microscope, she saw the fungus's hyphae deep inside the bat's wing tissue. In fact, the hyphae had destroyed and replaced areas of the dermis, the living skin tissue of the bat's wing. The fungus had even destroyed the blood vessels and nerves in that wing tissue.

With light shining through the wing, Meteyer saw the bat's wing bones. However, in some places, blood vessels that should've been weaving through the wing tissue were missing.

The discovery shocked Meteyer. "My palms started to sweat when I realized how the fungus was attacking the bats," she said. "I simply never expected to see that kind of damage to the wing tissue."

Meteyer examined one hundred more bats. She looked at dead bats from different caves and mines—even different states. The results were always the same. Big sections of dermis tissue had been dissolved and replaced by the fungi's hyphae. This fungus was clearly having a big impact on the wings of any bat it infected.

Could that damage be enough to kill a bat?

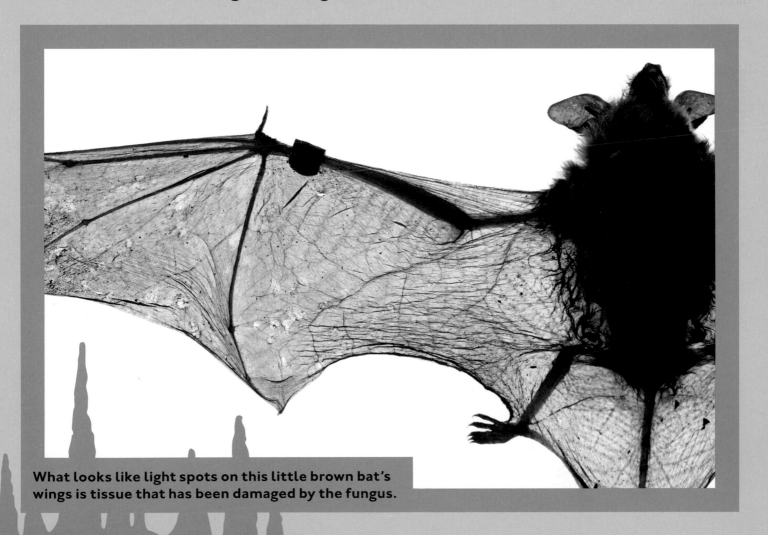

What looks like light spots on this little brown bat's wings is tissue that has been damaged by the fungus.

More than three-fourths of all the skin on a bat's body is covering its wings.

A Bat's Special Wings

In a healthy bat, the wing skin is thin, soft, and elastic. To get an idea what healthy bat wing skin is like, close your eyes and gently stroke your eyelids.

A bat's wings are made up of much more than skin, though. Two layers of skin surround a framework of bones and muscles, plus connective tissue and a web of nerves and blood vessels. This makes the wings key to controlling a bat's body temperature. With its wings spread out, a bat quickly loses body heat. With its wings wrapped around itself, a bat traps body heat. And a bat's body loses water through its wings too—a little when they're folded up and a lot more when they're spread out.

By studying the fungi's life cycle, scientists learned this new kind of fungus grew only in cold environments. That meant it was perfectly suited to attack hibernating bats. Normally, cells and organs of an animal's immune system work to fight off infections. However, studies of other hibernating animals had shown that during hibernation, the immune system slows down, meaning it isn't as active in attacking fungi, bacteria, or viruses. Meteyer reasoned that a hibernating bat's immune system would do the same thing. Her discovery proved that once a bat was infected, the fungus seriously damaged its wings.

Based on these facts, scientists concluded this new fungus was the reason bats were dying. But unlike a deadly virus, this fungus wasn't the direct cause of death. Instead, it might irritate the bats enough to cause them to come out of hibernation. Or it might speed up water loss

These bats died when they flew out of their hibernation site and into a winter storm.

through the wing tissue so the bats needed to become active and drink more often than normal. Whatever the reason, the fungus made the bats come out of hibernation over and over during the winter. That made the bats use up their stored fat too fast. Weak from hunger, some of the infected bats flew out of their hibernation site in search of food before there was any available. Then some froze to death in fierce winter weather. Others became easy prey for predators, like hawks. Still others starved to death.

Because of the damage this fungus caused, NWHC director David Blehert and his team gave the new fungus the scientific name *Geomyces destructans*. But studies of its DNA later proved it could not be classified as a type of *Geomyces*. So its name was officially changed to *Pseudogymnoascus destructans* (soo-doh-jim-no-ASK-us dis-TRUK-tans). It's also known as *Pd*.

Bats infected with this fungus appear to have fuzzy white noses. So scientists named the disease caused by the fungus white-nose syndrome.

Where Did *Pd* Come From?

After Al Hicks sent other researchers the photo of the bats with fuzzy white noses, he heard back from a scientist in France. Hicks learned that for years, bat researchers there had seen a white fuzzy growth on bats from time to time. He later heard similar reports from other parts of Europe. However, not many hibernating European bats were dying from white-nose syndrome. So once the NWHC team identified the fungus as deadly in North America, scientists wondered if it was really the same fungus. David Blehert's team partnered with a team at the Leibniz Institute for Zoo and Wildlife Research in Berlin, Germany. Together, the teams studied DNA taken from the fungus growing on both North American and European bats. The results of these tests confirmed that the same fungus—*Pseudogymnoascus destructans*—was attacking bats in both parts of the world.

David Blehert works in his lab in Wisconsin.

27

European bats, like these greater mouse-eared bats hibernating in Germany, are less likely to die from white-nose syndrome than North American bats.

Identifying the fungus wasn't the end of the mystery. The discovery of this deadly new fungus that attacks deep, living skin cells left scientists with two new questions: Could *Pd* be stopped from killing bats? And could bats survive long enough for that to happen?

Pd was killing lots of North American bats but having little effect on European bats. Scientists suspect that might be partly because North American bats had never before been exposed to this fungus. European bats, meanwhile, may have adapted to it. Scientists think that long ago, the fungus may have hit European bats hard. Those alive today are likely to be descendants of the survivors, who must have passed along genes for traits that help bats survive infection from white-nose syndrome. So modern European bats may have a natural resistance. The kinds of bats living in Europe are also generally larger than little brown bats and other kinds of North American bats. Being bigger might help lessen the impact of the infection. In addition, European bats tend to hibernate in groups of no more than a few hundred. Many kinds of North American bats hibernate in groups of as many as fifty thousand or more. Such large groups let the fungus spread quickly to lots of bats. Environmental conditions in Europe also may just be different enough to give the bats an advantage. European bats tend to hibernate for shorter periods, so the fungus doesn't have as long to attack before the bats' immune system kicks in.

Of course, there could be yet another factor helping European bats survive *Pd*. Scientists hope to learn how European bats are able to live with *Pd* in time to help North American bats survive in the same way.

The Race Is On

Pseudogymnoascus destructans is spreading from east to west across North America. People exploring caves in North America after hiking in Europe may have first carried *Pd* spores on their boots into these sites. But infected bats are likely continuing to spread it.

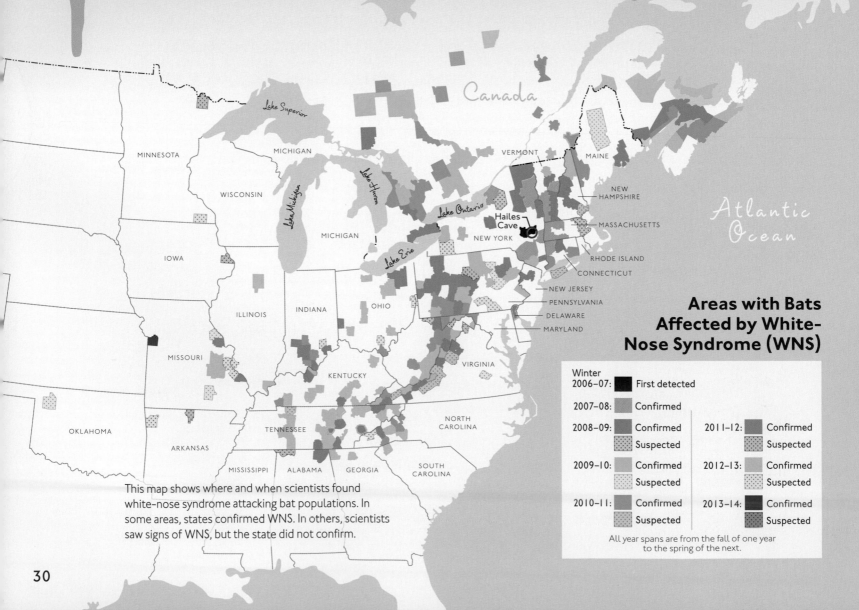

This map shows where and when scientists found white-nose syndrome attacking bat populations. In some areas, states confirmed WNS. In others, scientists saw signs of WNS, but the state did not confirm.

Areas with Bats Affected by White-Nose Syndrome (WNS)

Winter			
2006–07:	First detected		
2007–08:	Confirmed		
2008–09:	Confirmed	2011–12:	Confirmed
	Suspected		Suspected
2009–10:	Confirmed	2012–13:	Confirmed
	Suspected		Suspected
2010–11:	Confirmed	2013–14:	Confirmed
	Suspected		Suspected

All year spans are from the fall of one year to the spring of the next.

In 2007 only a few sites in New York State were infected. By 2013 *Pd* had been discovered at many sites across twenty-two states plus five Canadian provinces. And white-nose syndrome is likely to continue spreading to more species of hibernating bats.

While the bats are active, their warm body temperatures keep the fungus in check. The trouble begins once the bats go into hibernation and cool to the temperature at which *Pd* thrives.

Looking ahead, scientists are worried about *Pd* spreading into the Rocky Mountains and beyond—something likely to happen in the not too distant future. Then even more kinds of bats that hibernate in that area during the winter are likely to be hit by white-nose syndrome.

In 2009 scientists checked the wings of dead bats found in Pennsylvania. They found that *Pd* had arrived.

Scientists are working hard to stop *Pd* or at least to help bats survive being infected by this fungus.

Before white-nose syndrome struck, DeeAnn Reeder studied how a bat's body functions. Once she learned about the fungus, she began trying to figure out how to help bats survive *Pd* during hibernation. First, she decided to test and confirm whether hibernation affects how well a bat's immune system can tackle *Pd*.

Reeder turned large environmental chambers, used to grow plants in controlled conditions, into artificial caves. Some were kept at 39°F (4°C) and some at 49°F (9°C). There also was one large flight cage kept warmer, at about 68°F (20°C). Reeder collected little brown bats and big brown bats for her test. Into each chamber and the flight cage, she placed healthy bats, bats with wounds showing infection from *Pd*, and bats suspected of being infected. All had special instruments called data loggers glued to their bodies. For nine weeks, the data loggers recorded the bats' body temperatures every thirty minutes. Reeder also observed how often the bats woke up and became active and how quickly, if at all, any skin wounds from *Pd* healed. These tests showed that bats in the coldest environment spent more time hibernating and that their wounds were the slowest to heal. In the end, all the test bats were rewarded by being warmed up, fed, and allowed to fully recover.

The data logger attached to each bat's back is about the size of an M&M candy.

Because of Reeder's findings, one team of scientists at the NWHC, led by David Blehert, is using instruments to monitor and record the temperature and humidity in caves in the eastern United States. Those caves include places where white-nose syndrome wiped out a large number of bats. They also include caves where white-nose syndrome wasn't reported until 2012 and 2013 and caves that are still fungus-free. The team wants to learn at what temperature and humidity *Pd* has the biggest impact on the hibernating bats. Then scientists may be able to find ways to change airflow patterns inside hibernation sites, altering the temperature and humidity. Their goal is to keep conditions just at the point that's okay for bats to hibernate but not perfect for *Pd* to grow. They hope that will slow *Pd* growth enough that bats can survive hibernation. Then, once the bats are active again, their immune systems can tackle the fungus.

DeeAnn Reeder and her colleague Greg Turner check the data downloaded from the bat's data loggers.

Meanwhile, DeeAnn Reeder has kept working on a way to help hibernating bats. Other scientists had already discovered that a chemical called Terbinafine kills fungi. In fact, this chemical is the active ingredient in a medicine used to treat athlete's foot in people. Reeder's team is working on developing an implant that attaches to a bat's back and slowly releases Terbinafine into the bat's blood. The key is to use just enough to kill the fungus without harming the bat.

"Of course," Reeder said, "even if we're successful, such chemical treatment will only work for small groups of bats, like those being kept alive in zoos. . . . We'd only want to use this treatment to keep some kinds of bats from becoming extinct. And we'd want to keep the surviving population alive until it could safely be returned to the wild."

A scientist checks on a bat receiving Terbinafine to see if it is still *Pd*-free.

Scientist Winifred Frick and her team are searching for a way to help save large populations of bats, like little brown bats, in their wild homes. The researchers want to find bacteria or fungi that might naturally stop the growth of *Pd*. They culture the fungus in big refrigerators. Then they introduce bacteria and other microbes they collect by swabbing healthy bats in infected caves, and they study how the microbes and the fungus interact. Their hope is that the healthy bats are survivors and that microbes on the bats' bodies helped them resist infection.

Scientists swab a healthy bat in a *Pd*-infected cave.

"We're having some luck with this," Frick said. "However, once we find helpful microbes, we're still a long way from figuring out how to apply them to bats in the wild."

Winifred Frick's team is thinking about creative solutions to this problem. One possibility is setting up sprayers at cave entrances. Bats swarming in and out of their summer daytime roosts would trigger these. Then the bats would fly through a mist of helpful microbes. If this method works, it could be used anywhere to protect the bats from *Pd* as they settle down to hibernate for the winter.

This little brown bat roosted in a cave during the daytime. Now it's flying in search of insect prey.

Some Little Brown Bats Help Themselves

In 2011, when Kate Langwig found hibernating little brown bats in the Adirondack mountain cave, it was a surprise. Langwig also made another discovery there. She found that some bats were hibernating solo. Usually little brown bats huddle together to hibernate. "Whether by chance or by choice, this is keeping the survivors safe," Langwig said.

The *Pd* fungus has wiped out more than 80 percent of all the little brown bats in many hibernation sites in eastern North America. However, Langwig doesn't believe the bats she discovered hibernating solo are doing that just because there are fewer bats around. Their changed behavior appears to be helping them. Langwig found that fewer little brown bats hibernating alone died from *Pd* than bats hibernating in groups.

"This gives me hope western bat populations won't be as hard hit by *Pd* when it arrives," she said. "In the West, bats already don't tend to hibernate in such tightly packed groups."

Like bats hibernating solo, bats hibernating in cooler and drier sites were less likely to become infected by *Pd*.

Will the Future Be Safe?

On a warm summer night in the United States, you're still likely to see a little brown bat swoop through the air to catch insects. However, to the east of the Appalachian Mountains, you won't see a bat as often as before. There are simply far fewer bats than there once were. Many kinds of bats that hibernate during the winter have died. Populations of little brown bats have been especially hard hit.

Their loss affects all the other animals that share their habitat. For one thing, their young are a food source for predators like snakes and martens. In addition, adult little brown bats control insect populations. The huge number of insects they eat helps minimize the spread of diseases such as West Nile fever and also lessens insect damage to plant crops. So farmers miss having such large populations of little brown bats patrolling the nighttime sky. We all do.

Each winter *Pd* kills more adult bats, and every summer, the remaining mature females produce only one pup each. Does this shrinking population mean that one day little brown bats, once one of the most common bats in North America, will completely vanish? Scientists are working very hard not to let that happen. For now, though, these bats are still in danger of being gone forever.

Some little brown bats still hibernate in *Pd*-free sites. Scientists hope to find a way to keep them safe from the spreading, deadly fungus.

43

Author's Note

In writing this book, I was impressed and inspired hearing firsthand from scientists about their efforts to save little brown bats and other kinds of bats. They've dared to wonder and pushed hard to test their ideas as they've worked to solve the mystery of what's killing the bats. The stakes are extremely high—keeping little brown bats and a number of other kinds of bats from becoming extinct. And scientists continue to collect clues in this ongoing investigation.

On a more personal note, as I've developed and written books over the years, one of my goals has been to inspire young readers to consider science careers. Researching this book became special for me during an interview with one scientist. She said that reading my books as a student was one of the early sparks that ignited her interest in working in science! That was great motivation for me to keep researching and writing. But the biggest motivation is that the world is full of science mysteries that need tackling. Any of you readers could grow up to be part of the next generation of science detectives. Then you too could be working to make this world a better place for all Earth's animals, including little brown bats.

Little Brown Bats Are Amazing!

Little Brown Bats are highly valued for being insect eaters with BIG appetites. During a summer evening, a single little brown bat can easily eat 0.1 to 0.3 ounces (4 to 8 grams) of insects. That's the weight of about one thousand mosquito-sized insects! Check out these other impressive facts about little brown bats:

- They may live a very long life—sometimes more than thirty years.

- They're skilled flyers, flying as fast as 21 miles (34 kilometers) per hour while hunting. As well as grabbing prey with their mouths, little brown bats scoop insects out of the air with their tail or wing membranes and then flick them into their mouths.

- They have thirty-eight teeth, all sharp (including the molars!) to help them grab and hold onto the hard-bodied insects they catch and eat.

- Babies cling to their mother's fur and, for a few days, even ride along during hunting trips. They're ready to be independent when they're only about a month old.

Help Your Local Bats

Here are some things you and your family can do for your local bats:

- Be bat friendly. One of the most important things you can do for bats is to leave them alone. If bats move into your attic or garage, call someone you can count on to gently remove the bats and set them free. Also stay out of places where bats are known to hibernate during the winter. That way you won't disturb the bats or risk spreading the *Pd* fungus.

- Build a bat house. On their website, Bat Conservation International supplies step-by-step instructions for building your local bats a home: http://www.dec.ny.gov/docs/administration_pdf /batbox.pdf. Pay close attention to the instructions for where to hang your completed bat house.

- Plant for little brown bats. Check with local conservation groups to find out if little brown bats live in your area. There's a good chance they do. Little brown bats hunt insects at night. So to help the bats, plant scented herbs and night-blooming flowering plants that will attract insects. Whether you plant in pots or a garden, good choices include evening primrose, sweet rocket, lemon balm, and mint. Check with a local nursery for the kinds of plants likely to grow well in your area.

- Protect bat habitats. Go online or check with local conservation groups to discover what kind of habitat bats in your area live in. Help make others aware of the importance of those areas, of preventing construction on those sites, stopping changes to water drainage through those areas, and protecting those places from pollution.

Global Efforts to Help

Check out these worldwide efforts to help bats. You and your family may want to join one of these or put one of these ideas into action in your community.

Organization for Bat Conservation http://www.batconservation.org/drupal/
The Organization for Bat Conservation is a Michigan-based group that works to help protect bats around the world. If you live near Detroit, Michigan, you can visit the Bat Zone at the Cranbrook Institute of Science (Bloomfield Hills, Michigan) and get up-close looks at over 150 different kinds of bats. Their website also offers opportunities to sponsor rescued bats and participate in conservation projects. Don't miss the About Bats section, including the activity-packed Kids Page.

Bat Conservation International http://www.batcon.org/
This organization's website is packed with amazing bat photos, information, and the latest news about bat health. There are also opportunities for your family to join and share in efforts to protect bat populations around the world. Don't miss the All About Bats information section and Kidz Cave discovery activities.

Glossary

bacteria: single-celled living things that may be round, spiral, or rod-shaped

climate: the weather conditions, including temperature, rainfall, and wind that are characteristic of an area

conidia: a fungal spore (seedlike part of a fungus)

culture: a method for multiplying a bacteria or fungus by providing everything needed for growth

dermis: the layer of living skin cells below the epidermis, the surface layer. It may contain blood vessels, nerves, elastic fibers, sweat glands, and hair follicles, the living parts of hairs.

epidermis: the outer layer of skin cells that covers and protects the dermis

extinct: no longer in existence

fungus: a group of living things that cannot make their own food and live by feeding on other organisms, living or dead. Fungi lack true roots, stems, or leaves, and they reproduce by spreading spores.

Geomyces: a group of threadlike fungi noted for having distinct conidia. They're able to break down tissue made of a tough material called keratin—what's found in skin and fingernails or claws.

hibernation: an inactive state in which animals avoid a period when conditions are unfavorable and food is largely unavailable

hyphae: branching rootlike parts of a fungus

immune system: a group of organs, tissues, and cells that work together to protect the body from disease-causing organisms, such as bacteria, fungi, and viruses

pathologist: someone who studies what causes diseases, how they develop, and what effect they have on hosts

pesticide: a chemical used to kill insects or other pests that harm plants, animals, or people

pollution: the introduction of something harmful into an environment

predator: an animal that catches and kills other animals for food

prey: an animal hunted and killed for food

Pseudogymnoascus destructans (Pd): a kind of fungus that grows between about 39°F and 59°F (4°C and 15°C). *Pd* moves between cells in the epidermis of hibernating bats and breaks down dermis cells. It was originally believed to be a type of *Geomyces* called *Geomyces destructans*. *Pd* is the cause of white-nose syndrome.

spore: a single-celled reproductive unit

virus: tiny genetic material that multiplies within a host's cells and often causes symptoms that make the host sick

Digging Deeper

To keep on investigating little brown bats and other kinds of bats, explore these books and websites:

Books
Carney, Elizabeth. *National Geographic Readers: Bats.* Washington, DC: National Geographic Children's books, 2010.
Read about different kinds of bats from around the world.

Carson, Mary Kay. *The Bat Scientists.* Boston: Houghton Mifflin Books for Children, 2010.
Explore along with scientists as they go into caves to study bats. See how Dr. Merlin Tuttle is joining in the investigation of WNS.

Markle, Sandra. *Bats: Biggest! Littlest!* Honesdale, PA: Boyds Mills Press, 2013.
Discover how a bat's size, whether it's large or small, and certain big and little features enable a bat to be successful in its natural habitat.

———. *Outside and Inside Bats.* New York: Atheneum, 1997.
Take an in-depth look at a bat's body and how it works.

Websites
Bat Sounds
http://www.batsaboutourtown.com/pages/BatSounds.htm
Listen to the sounds made by little brown bats. Compare the sounds made by a number of other bats. Also check out information about each of the bats.

Countdown to Extinction for Little Brown Bat
http://www.bu.edu/today/2010/countdown-to-extinction-for-little-brown-bat/
This video takes you inside caves alongside scientists to see how white-nose syndrome is affecting the little brown bat.

Little Brown Bats
http://www.squidoo.com/little-brown-bat
Explore all kinds of activities to learn more about bats, especially little brown bats.

Little Brown Bat Stretches and Yawns Before Taking a Nap
http://www.youtube.com/watch?v=AxExwByOb9c&feature=related
Check out a video showing how a bat moves and uses its wings.

Index

Photo Acknowledgments

The images in this book are used with the permission of: © iStockphoto.com/cheri131, pp. 1, 3, 4 (top), 6 (top), 9, 18, 30 (top), 42, 44, 47; © Carl Heilman II/Wild Visions, Inc., pp. 4 (bottom), 18–19, 19 (top); © Minden Pictures/SuperStock, p. 5; © Laura Westlund/Independent Picture Service, pp. 6 (bottom), 30 (bottom); © Stephen Alvarez/National Geographic Stock, pp. 7 (top), 12–13, 21, 23, 31, 36–37; Nancy Heaslip, New York State Department of Environmental Conservation, p. 7 (bottom); US Fish and Wildlife Service/Ann Froschauer, pp. 8, 22; Alan Hicks, New York State Department of Environmental Conservation, pp. 8–9, 41; US Fish and Wildlife Service/Tim Krynak, pp. 10–11; US Fish and Wildlife Service, p. 15; AP Photo/Amy Smotherman Burgess, Knoxville News Sentinel, pp. 16, 38, 42–43; Ryan von Linden, New York State Department of Environmental Conservation, p. 17 (top); Melissa Behr, D.V.M., Wisconsin Veterinary Diagnostic Laboratory, University of Wisconsin–Madison, p. 17 (bottom); Wibbelt G, et al. White-nose syndrome fungus (*Geomyces destructans*) in bats, Europe. *Emerg Infect Dis 2010* 16(8):1237–1242, p. 19 (bottom); AP Photo/Mike Groll, p. 20; © Joe McDonald/CORBIS, pp. 24, 39; Kevin Wenner/Pennsylvania Game Commission, p. 25; US Fish and Wildlife Service/Marvin Moriarty, p. 26; US Geological Survey/photo by Cathy Acker, p. 27; © Martin Gabriel/naturepl.com, p. 28; Greg Turner/Pennsylvania Game Commission, p. 33; Joe Kosack/Pennsylvania Game Commission, p. 35.

Cover photographs © Animals Animals/SuperStock (main); © iStockphoto.com/cheri131 (jacket flap).